LETTERS FROM DARKNESS

LETTERS FROM DARKNESS

Poems by
DANIELA CRĂSNARU

Translated by
FLEUR ADCOCK

Oxford   New York
OXFORD UNIVERSITY PRESS
1991

Oxford University Press, Walton Street, Oxford OX2 6DP
Oxford   New York   Toronto
Delhi   Bombay   Calcutta   Madras   Karachi
Petaling Jaya   Singapore   Hong Kong   Tokyo
Nairobi   Dar es Salaam   Cape Town
Melbourne   Auckland
and associated companies in
Berlin   Ibadan

Oxford is a trade mark of Oxford University Press

Poems in Part I are selected in agreement with the author
from the original Romanian published collections:
Niagara de Plumb © Daniela Crăsnaru 1984 (Editura Eminescu)
and Emisferele de Magdeburg © Daniela Crăsnaru 1987 (Cartea Românească)

First published as an
Oxford University Press paperback 1991

British Library Cataloguing in Publication Data
Data available

Library of Congress Cataloging in Publication Data
Crăsnaru, Daniela.
[Poems. English. Selections]
Letters from darkness: poems/by Daniela Crăsnaru: translated by Fleur Adcock.
p. cm. —(Oxford poets)
1. Crăsnaru, Daniela—Translations, English. I. Adcock, Fleur.
II. Title. III. Series.
PC840.13.R34A23 1991 859'.134—dc20 91-9839

ISBN 0-19-282883-5

Typeset by Wyvern Typesetting Ltd.
Printed in Hong Kong

ACKNOWLEDGEMENTS

Some of these versions have appeared in the *Honest Ulsterman, Illuminations, Oxford Poetry, Poetry Review*, and the *Times Literary Supplement*. Six of the poems from Part II were published in *The Independent on Sunday*.

I should like to thank Oana Lungescu for reading through parts of my manuscript in draft and giving me useful advice.

Oxford University Press acknowledges the financial assistance of the Arts Council of Great Britain towards the publication of this volume of translations.

FOREWORD

DANIELA CRĂSNARU was born in Craiova, Romania, in 1950, and studied Romanian and English at Craiova University. She has published twelve collections of poetry as well as children's books, and lives in Bucharest with her husband and daughter. Before the revolution she was an editor with the Eminescu Publishing House, but had to take early retirement, partly because of poor health and partly because of difficulties with her editor-in-chief, who objected to the fact that she consistently refrained from censoring manuscripts which came to her for editing. She was made to stand up at staff meetings and face accusations of having done no work, because the texts she had passed for publication were not criss-crossed with blue ink. For these offences she was punished by cuts in her salary, and in the end she left. However, after the fall of Ceauşescu she was appointed director of Editura Ion Creanga, a firm which publishes children's books. She still works there, but in addition she is now a member of parliament: she was elected in May 1990 as an 'independent', appearing on the list of the National Salvation Front but not a member of that party.

Her poetry has been highly praised by the critics. Like all Romanian poets writing under censorship she adopted the device of shrouding her work heavily in metaphors and imagery, but this did not conceal from her fellow-writers and other discerning readers its subtext of hostility towards state institutions and what was being inflicted on the people. Her books continued to be published, with an increasing number of deletions, but she was regarded with suspicion by the authorities.

During the second half of the 1980s she wrote, in addition to the 'public' poems, a series of secret ones which she kept hidden in her aunt's cellar, in a box under some onions, because her own flat was liable to be searched. After the revolution she wrote to me saying 'Now I am free to send you my real poems.' ('Real' in this context means honest or truthful; her earlier work, with its tense subtleties, is nonetheless real as artistic achievement.)

Part I of this collection consists of poems published in Romania before December 1989; most are from two of Daniela Crăsnaru's recent books, *Niagara de Plumb* (Editura Eminescu, 1984) and *Emisferele de Magdeburg* (Cartea Românească, 1987).

'Pietà' (in memory of her father) appeared in the journal *România Literară* in 1988. Part II contains a selection of the secret poems. *Letters from Darkness* is her own title for them.

FLEUR ADCOCK
London, December 1990

CONTENTS

I PUBLISHED POEMS

PIETÀ

Almost a year; Gemini in the ascendant
and not a sign of you.
Your body, washed by subterranean tears,
is a palimpsest written by my memory:
first the gritted consonants
then, in a haze, the vowels.
What did they say, the architects of the underworld,
when they saw your shrunken body,
your scars, your broken veins?
Have they taken you too for a ride on their Circle Line
from being towards Nature?
Have they shown you yet
the great hall of the Elements?
What are you doing there,
added to the mineral silence
as, at another time,
you were part of the shouting in great stadiums?
Have your eyes got used to the signs of darkness?
Can you decipher yet the Morse code of rain?

Are you now one of theirs?

Almost a year and Gemini's in the ascendant:
an air-sign.
How would it be translated to you, where you are?
Or how would these words of mine
smelling more and more of earth?

SIMPLE RHYMES

Inside the space behind my brow
nothing's happened for ages now.

It's a flat smooth plain without a ridge:
a desert; and there's a narrow bridge

across which trails a meek procession
of words with saintly self-possession;

none of them shouts or gets out of line
in this fantasy paradise of mine

constructed according to tidy schemes
without mutiny, teeth-gnashing or dreams,

my flat smooth desert without a ridge
approached by a very narrow bridge.

One false step, and down to perdition
they go, the words that leave their position —

the lively rebels in disgrace,
the words which haven't found their place
or are stuck in one they just can't face:

for them I've opened down below
(but only in my mind, you know)
an abattoir where the bad words go.

Such consonant-butchery, such slaughter —
blue blood sloshing around like water

under the narrow bridge they tread
to the small Siberia in my head.

POSSIBLE DEFINITION

Let me write about reality
with my eyes closed: that's to say,
driven back into the ivory tower
which (here we go—smash, bash!)
I have just demolished.
I am a highly qualified worker
in the imaginative illusions factory,
a team-leader on the ineffable
production-line of superlatives.

Look, you hopes, you iron crags!
Witness the birth, in your name,
of my rebellious and candid words
wrapped in their grey caul
complete with brains, complete with me,
with my blood in the veins of their vowels;
and look who's waltzing towards them:
the Chief of Sanitation
with a spray-can of perfumed air-freshener
and the Head of Decorative Art
with some new embroidery designs.

Look, you intact hopes, you iron crags!
In your name, in the name of that chronic
optimism which is our salvation,
I continue to refuse this favour,
this free ticket for a journey
conducted by dirigible
from which everything is seen
on a scale of one to 23 million;
in your name I shall continue
to write about reality
which continues to be the way it is.

ORPHIC

I dreamed I was working as a servant
in a lion-pit:
that's to say, I did the cleaning, I fed the beasts—
of my own accord, from my palm;
yes, from the hand with which I caress my child;
of my own accord, from the hand with which I write
that luminous, calm poetry.

I've dreamt the same thing many times over;
I've got used to that incomprehensible dream,
just as I've got used to myself;
just as you get used to noise,
to lack of love,
to absurdly repeated questions
which don't receive an answer.

Curious that the dream recurs identically.
I know at every second that the terror is false,
that it's written into the scenario
that nothing will happen to me,
that my servitude in the lion-pit would vanish
like a puff of smoke
if I could lift an eyelid.

In the morning things appear just as before.
I myself am probably the same;
it's only that for some time now I haven't known
whether the hand which at night holds bleeding meat
is actually the hand with which I write.

6

THE WINDOW IN THE WALL

Up against the wall, as close as possible,
with my hands flat against it, my face glued to it,
my breath returning into my nostrils,
weighed down by humid darkness—
one step, one day; another step, another day—
it must be here.
Yes, here it *is*, the window,
its grey rectangle.

With my hands full of chalk I stroke the pane
as I would stroke your shoulders, your thighs.
What a cheap, stagy light would come from outside,
what a tumult of scorching sap!
Think what I can invent in your absence:
a cloudburst of rain; an English park
through which hunting-dogs run
with enormous bounds;
the sky, its grey slab
supported by my own breath;
a hillock in the background
ignoring all the laws of classical perspective;
a graveyard of lead invaded
by tiny, plaintive interjections.
So much else could be on the other side of the window
which I have not the courage to break
if I can't open it—
this window I clumsily drew
myself with chalk
on the wall.

PASTEL

It smells of winter—
of rotting wood, of the dark, of tears
whose rounded ends are little spheres;
a slow current where poisons flow
into what was pure—best not to know;
a life stopped suddenly in a vein,
a wound opened without pain,
a scream stifled in bales of floss,
a new loss added to loss.
It smells of fear, of plants that will die;
it smells of earth smeared over the sky.

DARWINISM

I can no longer write.
They've put a patch
on my brain.
They've put an umbrella on my brain.

Its spokes
piercing deeper and deeper
through my veins
divide the noble matter
into precise sections.

I feel no pain, I don't suffer,
but
if only it would rain!
At least let someone stand with a watering-can
over the leading man
so that both they and I may have
a justification,
now
when the damp words
are just climbing on to the dry land of paper,
are just learning to drag themselves along
through the white desert
acquiring new auxiliary organs.

Even those new organs
frighten me
with their astonishing capacity
for adaptation.

VAMPIRIAD (I)

With my own hands I made it,
that unique vessel;
with my own breath
I perfected all its curves
like the most celebrated
master glass-blower
until life pulsed in its veins
more and more faintly; scarcely a flicker.
'What a funny gift' says my lover,
and taps lightly on the thin glass;
he taps it with his hand
to check on its quality,
to see if it's worth
even a glance.
'Ah' he says, accepting the gift,
smashing it to splinters,
to smithereens,
'be a good girl; do me a favour
and step on them with your bare feet—
like this, darling; yes, that's the way.
But be careful now, and smile too,
and above all don't bleed!'

VAMPIRIAD (II)

He says:
'Take care not to catch cold;
and even the green signal
at the traffic-lights
is sometimes misleading.
This autumn
could burn your eyes
with its red foliage.
You see that I suffer if you suffer.
Take care to keep fit—
fly for several hours a day;
buy yourself two woollen scarves;
and above all don't die, don't die.
Be careful about phosphates,
iron, the electrolytic balance;
avoid darkness, fear,
emotions, and in general
everything you think could do you
any harm.
You know that one day, very soon,
I shall certainly need
a total exchange transfusion
of your blood.
But now keep calm, relax,
and ask me any question you like.'
– 'Do you love me?'
– 'No.'

THE LOST WAR

He has lost his perfect athlete's body;
his temples ring with a bitter clang.
He is no longer the fore-ordained winner
but merely the dice he himself has flung.

He is eternally a subject,
apathetic, bored by his own state;
he is, very occasionally,
my grieving body's predicate.

All the battles seem to be won
and yet the war is lost in advance.
He moves, without knowing it, laughing and burning
through this circle of words, which binds

and constricts him like an outgrown coat
he is forced to wear from time to time.
He is my devouring fiction
and the sad blood of many a poem.

AUTUMN POEM

I'm nostalgic for a past autumn,
with its smell of woods
with life surging through the leaves
towards the roots, into the ground—
a bitter autumn, truly experienced
more in the soul, more
in language.
This present autumn
smells of death
of cardboard scenery and of falseness.
This autumn,
my soul, do you know what it is?
It is a dress rehearsal
for an autumn which once occurred
and of which I have forgotten
the key speech.

IMAGE OF A CHILDHOOD AND A
HORSE IN WORLD WAR II

Every night I wander
through great horse-fairs
from England to Asia Minor,
but that particular horse
I can't find anywhere.
I'd give anything to buy it for you
and bring it back to you—
stunned adolescent on the hill
at Z,
seen in passing from a car
after almost fifty years,
still there in the negative
of that image of two soldiers
taking the rein from your hands,
your frightened
adolescent hands
(I love the way your hands were then).
How it stays on my retina,
the imprint of that image
which I have never seen!
Far more than all the films
about the war, with their gallons
of crimson paint;
far more than all the books.
That sequence like a supreme
definition of loss
is not part of my own memory
but has been added to it
like the hot slash of a
bayonet through a life-line—
horse and childhood diminishing
in darkness, in the basalt
underground of memory;
two nameless soldiers
for the sake of boundless vanity . . .
From Asia Minor to England
I wander now night after night
through great horse-fairs

as far as the vague rim
of morning,
as far as the edge of that
hill at Z, almost
fifty years ago,
which has never belonged and never
will belong to me, even
in my memory,
but which has been added to it
definitively
like a burning scar
through the life-line.

INDIGO, VIOLET

In the horse's belly
the Greeks drink wine and prepare themselves
for victory.
Before the last day
the Trojans don't know
that tomorrow is the last day.
The Thirty Years' War
is also in its thirtieth year;
on the penultimate day
of the thirtieth year
its soldiers, too, don't know
that tomorrow is the last day.
The Hundred Years' War
is in its ninety-ninth year;
on the last day
of the ninety-ninth year
its soldiers likewise
don't know that today is the last day—
and yet
the smell of death is evident
from miles away:
the smell of death,
as close to the smell of love
as violet to indigo
in the spectrum of light.

In front of your heart
a stone dial,
a minute-hand
which very soon
will also turn to stone.

Indigo, violet:
the smell of love and the smell of death,
two twin butterflies
in a chrysalis of clay.

In front of your heart
a stone dial, a minute-hand
turned to stone.

Not today, not today, perhaps *tomorrow*—
the word twisting in a final spasm
at the corner of clenched lips.
Tomorrow.
Purple dye, a trickle of blood
under the Pharaoh's perfect mask.

THE LIONS OF BABYLON

A morning
five thousand years ago.
In the stone cellars
of the palace,
to the left and right of the scribe,
the lions of Babylon.
He
has never seen the sun,
he hasn't seen the river,
hasn't seen the sea.
He is now bent over, writing
on a clay tablet
about the sun.
He gives a minutely detailed description
of how the great river flows
into the sea.
The slave who is dictating to him
has for his part also never
seen the river,
the sun, the sea. He too
has heard of them—
from another slave
who glued his whole body against a wall
until he lost his breath,
until he bled,
until his body caught
the light from outside,
the murmur of the river as it flowed
into the sea.

WRITING LESSON

I am going to fail my course.
The teacher says
'Describe this waterfall,
brilliant and majestic in the sunrise.'
I stand with my eyes popping
at the anaemic thread of water
trickling in the cracked gutter
and say humbly 'I can't,
I just can't.'
'You have no wings' says the teacher,
'and not a crumb of metaphysics.
Repeat now after me:
White, brilliance, light, crystal.
(Joy).'
White, brilliance—pretty words
with neatly starched lace collars
through which, alas, with such impertinence
feverish reality gushes
like blood through a sterilized bandage.

My final argument:
on the beach last summer
the farewell speech
of a drowned man dragged ashore
was just the stream of water
gushing from his lungs.
I saw it with my own eyes: not
immaculate petals, not
the fluttering of butterflies.
Water with blood in it running over the sand.

'You are going to fail your course'
says the teacher, and pushes me into space
from the seventh floor of the school.
He pretends not to see.
I pretend not to die.

FAIRYTALE IN FRAGMENTS

O, Hänsel, welche Not!

1

M for memory—minor melancholy,
marsupial pouch in which I lie
overcome by celestial juices:
poppy, nightshade, mandragora.
The drugs of the great astral conjunction—
red Mars, in the ascendant,
M the trident
thrust right into the core;
and I here, in balloons of helium,
on streets of chlorine, in rooms of mercury.
Keep on sprinkling millet, keep on sprinkling flour, oh
soror mea mors,
how shall we ever get back?
We're lost in the forest of signs, of seeds,
with a thousand gingerbread houses.
Hee-hee, ha-ha, give me your finger through the bars,
give me that fragile poem
which is no longer putting on weight;
light the furnace, its red blaze—
books burn; words don't.

2

M for magic. Meta-language. Hello = I love you
in an unknown tongue.
Memory, brief lightning-flash which shows you
horrifying openings, fissures. Out of them
come devilish incubi to surround you
with their cackling—
right now, when
birds and animals and showers
have wiped out all the tracks we laid down.
What's the use, why should we return?
Better stay here
in the melodious darkness,
in the consuming fire which has no Memory.

3
Snail-slow.
Day after day.
Fairy-tales in fragments, in smithereens
impossible to reconstruct. Dust
at the bottom of the drawing;
almost outside the frame,
a headless stalk of forget-me-not—
Myosotis. The eyes don't see it.
They don't recognize it. It doesn't hurt them.
On the white, deserted, aseptic streets
death scatters the alphabet.

SUNSET BOULEVARD

How my youth has passed, under all kinds of banner—
faded hopes, small questionings,
a soothing dialectic! Those fragile 'mannerist' poems
whose melancholy no longer annoys anyone.
(How talented she is, what a well-behaved child,
this fat little girl who must never, never, never
reach adolescence! Plastic flowers for the buttonhole
of this fragment of life set carefully on the shelves.)
Then the small revolt smelling of naive hope, of oxygen;
my eagerness to speak at last of certain things
by name. But 'What's in a name? That which we call a rose
by any other name would smell as sweet.'
Just so. There's a smell of darkness on the escalator
which carries me down to the basement of memory;
an automaton has taken my place, searching
in the dictionary of neologisms for better sentiments.
With great syringes of rainwater I wanted to cure
the leukaemia of this twilit motorway.
At the end of it waits the poem I breathe through,
the tired, cyanotic lung into which I pour molten lead.
How my youth has passed! Straight from the Young Hopefuls
to the Old Boys' Team: my puffed-out sadness scarcely fit
to wear a jersey at the local friendly match.
'Six landscape poems in a row are equal to six square metres
    of nature.'
Fiction, that enormous hammock. Heaven looks through its
    mesh,
as if through bars, at what's happening here on earth.
Then irony, the last chance, the burning glove with which I
    tried
to defuse the fat grenade stuffed with events.
The explosion—its hellish bang. The immense crater—the
    orbit
into which, one day, God
will boot all the other landscapes.

A BASKET OF CHERRIES

With this Sunday's non-winning lottery ticket in the drawer of
    noon
I try small levitation exercises, right now
when everything has the colour of lead heated
to a thousand degrees.
Youth, that stuffed canary
flying through the outer reaches of language.
Not a sign
from the body in which I live illicitly
like a travelling salesman with a sprained ankle.
On the field of Marathon weeds have grown,
while the lighthouse at the Cape of Good Hope
hands out tickets for the Amateur Blind Club.

On the screen of memory, in place of you,
a basket of cherries like monstrous cells—
voracious, bloody,
a still life in the expressionist style.
On the rotting surface of a wooden table
the bandage of a newspaper invaded by ants.
In the series 'The Novel of Love' Tristan and Isolde
on paper of 45-gram quality.

With the sword from page 180 I shred
this Sunday's non-winning lottery ticket.
With the boat from page 200
I try to cross the Sea.

LAST TRAIN

Fifteen minutes on Ciulniţa station
between two trains full of net-makers—
long enough to see in lonely women's eyes
how sadness brims up,
how it flows unchecked
into this noonday dust.
Praise be to you,
circulation systems in the blood,
that, who knows why, you do your duty;
and praise to you, aorta,
and to you, death-line on my palm!
A green light:
signal that anaesthesia is beginning,
that a layer of slime is settling
over the helpless flap of words in the brain.
'I-love-you-I-love-you'
while the wheels go mad,
while all the instincts recall their ambassadors
to coincide with the train's departure,
without me, for the sea.
'Slav sadness', you say,
running for cigarettes, for a mug of water
in the cheap bar,
for two small silver rabbits,
shot long ago, dead long ago.
'Slav sadness', you say from far away,
from behind a mountain suddenly reared up on the plain.

OXYGEN

I

Cloud like a strangling curl from the hair of Fate:
the gaze drinks it in, the eye fills with it
unconsciously.
Above a cover, above
the roof of the world
among all kinds of stony perils—
your eye and your hand won't obey you;
there's only your little glowing demon
the crystal of quartz
the lamp shining
in voluptuous darkness.

II

Letters. Letters which need you, need your life,
need your air
to cover this ice-cap
an abstract summit
a white expanse on which the traces you leave are
letters, letters, letters.
It's not wolves that come to track them, to savage them,
but your own future
hurled backwards
as if you were walking towards the past.

III

'I'm frightened' I say in the nitrogen of the second
which is smothering me.
'You're making a fuss' they say, turning on the chlorine tap,
putting on the voice of a mother, colouring in
scenes of childhood with water-paints—
my retina, my ear-drum, the bones of my ear
still function perfectly.
Get down, go on tiptoes,
stay on your knees!
Good, that's right. An anaerobic plant:
gather, cancel, wait.

IV

Short breaths, each one more laboured;
the sweaty border of tears.
Life in the capillaries—a market-place in uproar,
the traders in the temple, oh
bitterness.

Each word is a stain
on the flame which gave birth to it.

Soiled with ink as if with alien blood
this thought which writes itself.

V

Framed in the cover of a book,
framed in an open window, on the edge of it
like a character from Tolstoy
I stand
in the blaze of my red dress,
my body careless, insolent.
A pleasing image.
Down there, far below, a crowd of people and dogs:
shouts, firemen, outspread nets.
But no!
Let it burn.
A pleasing image.
But I have never had
a red dress.
But I am on the ground floor
grounded.

VI

With ever decreasing strength, up, right up
under the curl of the strangling cloud,
air scarce, breathing scarce.

To be hauled in flames
over that expanse, over the ice of the white page
not only breath
even your name falls from your body
irreversibly.

VII

Exemplary patient;
along the corridors of the occiput, into the grey
of the noble matter. Blind, deaf and without desires
on a trolley with wax wheels
trundled here into the depths
into the centre of pain.
Exemplary patient; imploding engine,
small fragile pistons beating fearfully
in capillaries ready to burst their mycelium.
Purple, purple, purple.
Sack of words like blind wriggling mice.
Sack of grey lead.
Exemplary patient. In pain? No pain.
Only the whole body breaks out in a rash
of speechless lips.

VIII

For a long time I believed that the back of this camel was
    the desert—
the imagination brutally inflating the feeble lungs
of the real with hallucinogenic shadows,
with beloved names, with superlatives.
The controlled effect of this abstract
weapon: my brain exploding.

IX

Strangling curl of hair,
cloud absorbed right down to the kidneys,
right down to your last written breath.
Oxygen, oxygen, oxygen.
Abstract tubes abruptly cut
by Her silver scissors.
Letters, letters,
like sunbeams on hayricks,
like young recruits on a train.
Mortal. Immortal.
Oxygen
oxygen
oxygen.

II LETTERS FROM DARKNESS

FAME

Writing poetry's no use!
'If you want to be famous in Europe
you must be at least a cannibal' said a poet friend
some years ago, when darkness, cold and hunger
were merely common nouns
from the basic vocabulary.
Now, this evening in February 1988,
the family is at supper around the gas-lamp.
Words freeze in the air. Tears freeze in the throat.
Three adults and a child.
On the child's fork, a fragment of meat.
'Perhaps she won't eat it all' each of us is thinking.
Today it's my turn to finish the leftovers.
We don't look at each other or speak to each other.
With frozen hands we spread jam on bread.
As yesterday, as tomorrow.
Tomorrow?
A simple adverb of time.
'Time is money?' asks the little girl.
No. For us time is fear.
With a primitive impulse I look humbly at the scraps of food
which today are for me. I look at my mother's thin hands,
my child's frail body.
'To be famous in Europe you must be at least a cannibal.'
That's not much to ask.
Fame is knocking at the door, in epaulettes and blood-stained
    stripes.
Europe will have a spectacle which it may not deserve.

MY PRIVATE HYDE PARK

By day I write poems that are obedient, quiet and
   publishable.
But at night I pull the blanket over my head,
close my eyes, and go off illicitly to Hyde Park—
a private Hyde Park in my tired brain—
and there I tell EVERYTHING to an enormous audience
of deaf-mutes who applaud me like mad.
Towards morning an angel comes: my personal angel
with a belt, a pistol, and a lot of stars on his shoulder.
'Hey, that's enough,' he says, 'the show's over;
who do you think you're impressing with your pathetic
   words?
Romania means nothing in the game of world politics:
an insignificant tract of land, a dusty annexe
of a great empire. A bagatelle.
Wake up and get into the queue for milk.'

Morning slashes the windows with its bloody knife.
And today I'll write quiet, obedient poems, full
of camouflaging metaphors. Publishable.
But first I'll iron my pillow
to dry out the tears; I'll erase the salty
shorthand record of my nocturnal speeches.
With a hot iron I'll press the damp surface of the pillow
like a criminal frantically removing traces of a crime.
And today, like yesterday, I'll begin my day
thinking up harmless synonyms
for Terror and Cowardice.

ORPHEUS IN THE UNDERWORLD

On the streets of Frankfurt, with a poet friend
who left Romania two years ago.
Light everywhere, advertisements, the smell of vanilla-
    flavoured sugar.
The superficial face of freedom.
'It's good here,' he says, 'I have enough to eat,
I can curse the government if I like, I can say anything out
    loud.
But I can't write poetry.
At home unhappiness was my chief source of inspiration.
The more unhappy you are, the better you write.
Suffering is the true material of poetry.'

I walk in silence beside him through the streets of this free
    city
and try to feel free, but I can't.
If his theory is correct
we Romanians have every prospect
of shortly becoming geniuses.

PRICE-LIST

'How much is a kilo of potatoes?'
'We haven't got any.'
'How much is a kilo of tomatoes?'
'We haven't got any.'
'How much is a gram of hope?'
'We haven't got any. But we can give you for nothing
a ton of tears from our great national stock-pile.'

SUPPLY AND DEMAND

Perhaps our only capital
is hope in God.
But we have no market economy;
we don't know the laws of supply and demand.
We no longer demand anything
because nothing is supplied.
So what could we do with this capital,
in this corner of the world
where misery is rigorously planned?
God is busy honouring
his own regulations:
'He that hath, to him shall be given, but he that hath not,
from him shall be taken even that which he hath.'
Both He and the Pope have an agenda
from which we've long been excluded.
In the end even God is a tourist,
free like other tourists to choose
happier and more luminous countries.

CHEESE!

I am 37 years old and they want me to write poems
not with words but with applause.
My hands will be sore, my knees will be sore
because they want me to applaud kneeling.
After all, what words are left
that we're still allowed to use in poems?
The word 'freedom' is forbidden.
The word 'oppression' is forbidden.
The word 'justice' is forbidden.
The word 'injustice' is forbidden.
The word 'democracy' is dangerous.
The word 'tyranny' doesn't exist.
The word 'love' is immoral.
Today is May the 10th. A day like any other.
A fine day. (I'm allowed to say that.)
I'd like to write a poem. It's 8 a.m. At this hour Mr Smith
is choosing between ham and eggs and coffee with milk and
    . . . It's hard to choose.
I look in the 'fridge and let out the word 'empty'.
So I have no dilemma.
At this hour M. Pierre, in Paris, doesn't know what kind of
    cheese
to choose, among the 37 available varieties.
'Cheese. What an archaism!' I say sadly.
'What's this? You're not allowed to remember!' warns my
    guardian angel.
'Be cheerful. Smile.'
'I can't. Have pity on me, leave me alone. Please!'
'I order you to smile. Say CHEESE!'

POLONIUS

I'm alone in this room
facing white sheets of paper
as if confronting a polar landscape.
Cold, doubt, insecurity.
And yet someone invisible
is listening, spying, making notes.
No one about. Doors locked. Shutters closed.
Only behind my words,
as if behind an enormous curtain,
Polonius is silently doing his duty.

LOVE POEM IN CAPTIVITY

They listen to everything.
They spy on everything.
They know everything.

I'm afraid of the furniture, the walls, the cat purring
on the cold radiator.
I'm afraid of friends, of my own child.
I'm afraid of myself.
On the telephone I talk about the weather,
about yesterday's football match.
About nothing.
I'd like to tell you, darling,
that I love you.
But I must be cautious
because who knows what *they* might think I meant by that?

CAMOUFLAGE POEM

I've learnt to be polite, efficient, obedient.
I've learnt to wait. I've learnt to stop waiting.
I've learnt to regard my word as ants, free
within their perimeter of paper, building abstract structures,
totally unaware of global and regional crises,
of emotional matters, ideas, and other fashionable drugs.
I've learnt to have courage.
Sometimes the courage to keep quiet, I've heard, is more
    important
than the courage to speak out. Sometimes not.
Choose!
I've learnt to choose. I've learnt to stop choosing.
So I swallow whole sentences, whole poems
as stoically as, when I was little, I swallowed codliver oil.
'Now then, don't cry,' she said, 'this'll make you big;
it makes you feel sick for a moment,
but get it down, and you'll see it'll do you good.'
I'd like to believe she was right. In time
codliver oil was replaced. In time
I got used to replacing words, too—
to constructing circumlocutions, finding synonyms.
Side by side with other poems, announcements,
    advertisements,
and whatever else can be found at a given moment
on a page (and this is a given moment)
my poems can scarcely be distinguished from them,
just as in a landscape you can scarcely pick out
the hunter's camouflage-clothing, the safari truck,
the lizard on a stone, etc., etc.
I ought to rejoice, to be pleased with myself;
I ought to remember my mother's voice—protective
and full of tenderness:
'It makes you feel sick for a moment,
don't cry, you'll see it'll do you good.'

OXFORD STREET

December in a foreign country.
A few days of freedom.
Do I deserve them, I wonder?
Perhaps my poems do.
In a square, a huge fir-tree.
'An annual Christmas gift from the people of Norway,'
explains my guide, a tall, blonde Englishwoman: typical.
But what else is typical today?
I mustn't think about anything. In particular,
I mustn't think about home.
We go into a cafe. My guide offers me
a 'Banana split'.
My daughter is seven years old and has never tasted bananas.
I'm ashamed of myself, of my poems—those soppy, meek,
apathetic poems which brought me here.
This Christmas too is going to be sad, chilly and poor,
I tell myself with a shudder, under the rain of multicoloured
    lights.
Words are running through my blood
like grenades full of tears.
'Oxford Street,' says my guide. 'Do you like it?'
'Yes, yes, how could I not?' I repeat politely
looking at the glossy stage-set of a reality
which is not mine,
that of a world of gingerbread and coloured balloons:
a world which rejects me like a foreign body, dark and
    humble.
Oxford Street. And me, with my wounds, with my violent
    blood,
with my painful and untranslatable experiences,
trying to give life to this huge fairy-tale tableau.

A PRIVATE AFFAIR

Where can I go?
My friend Gerhardt has relations in West Germany
and, God willing, he'll escape to them.
My friend Eva is Hungarian
and, God willing, she'll go to relations in Hungary
where the bars of the cage aren't quite so strong.
But what about me? Where can I go,
since my homeland is the Romanian language?
What became of Tarkovski and Solzhenitsin?
The West gets bored so quickly
with dissidents from the Third World.
How funny we are, aren't we? What a spectacle—
for a month, a year.
From the front page of the newspapers to the back,
then to the common grave of dead news.

Ladies and gentlemen!
These tears really are tears.
This blood is not red paint.
This life of mine is not a stunt;
no currency in the world can pay for it.
I know that everything's commercial:
love, friendship, freedom, art, beliefs—
they can all be bought and sold.
But even so I've a huge advantage:
here, where we live, death is still a private affair
for which I'm in training every day.

THE BEGINNING OF THE END

We eat the same food,
we have the same fears,
we think the same thoughts.
Instead of total love,
which in two thousand years we haven't succeeded in
    learning,
total hatred:
this is what unites us—
more and more mean,
more and more hungry,
more and more tired.
'That's good' a voice tells me—
I don't know whether it's the Devil's or the Angel's—
'that's very good indeed, because
this could be
the beginning of the end.'

PACT WITH THE DEVIL

He is eternally present;
he is waiting for my consent.
He doesn't offer me riches, or boundless pleasures,
or eternal youth.
He wants to sign up my poems for that anonymous choir
which extols disaster.
He wants my soul in exchange for tomorrow.
That's all he's offering me: tomorrow —
a grey, gloomy, amorphous day —
because this devil too is poor, powerless
and lacking a vocation;
an anonymous devil, conscientiously doing his duty.
He perseveres.
So do I.

NOLI TANGERE CIRCULOS MEOS

It seems to be an obvious fact
that we're in the twentieth century. In its final years.
So it is for you, dear citizens
of free Europe!
Here, though, time and space are different.
How right old Einstein was!
We're the proof that his theory's valid.
I read and write by a candle, like a century ago,
in the cold of a prehistoric cave.
Very soon they may take away from me
not only light, warmth and food.
These are just small superficial terrors, to which
I've become almost immune.
But soon they'll come right inside; they'll tramp in their
    barbaric boots
through my brain, into my spirit, into the divine part of me.
They'll ruin it as the Roman soldier
once ruined the diagrams of Archimedes.
'Noli tangere circulos meos!' I shout in despair.
'Not in here. NEVER!' I shout, covering my head with my
    hands
on to which flows like desperate blood
the ink of my powerless words.

STILL LIFE

'Cultivate the great, eternal themes—
love, birth, death.
Poetry of the moment hasn't a chance. It isn't literature.'
So says my friend who is afraid for me, for
tomorrow.
The truth? Which truth?
Who's interested in the truth?
Suffering, misery, pain, are not contagious
and not translatable.
The truth, perhaps, is this illicit June afternoon,
your hands caressing me sadly;
this corner of a table on which are lying a knife
and two slices of salami. Still life.
Heterogeneous objects
monstrously magnified
under the lens of this tear through which I see the world.

OXFORD POETS

Fleur Adcock
Edward Kamau Brathwaite
Joseph Brodsky
Basil Bunting
Daniela Crăsnaru
W. H. Davies
Michael Donaghy
Keith Douglas
D. J. Enright
Roy Fisher
David Gascoyne
Ivor Gurney
David Harsent
Gwen Harwood
Anthony Hecht
Zbigniew Herbert
Thomas Kinsella
Brad Leithauser
Derek Mahon

Medbh McGuckian
Jamie McKendrick
James Merrill
Sean O'Brien
Peter Porter
Craig Raine
Henry Reed
Christopher Reid
Stephen Romer
Carole Satyamurti
Peter Scupham
Penelope Shuttle
Louis Simpson
Anne Stevenson
George Szirtes
Grete Tartler
Edward Thomas
Charles Tomlinson
Chris Wallace-Crabbe

Hugo Williams